Fatty Liver Diet

Guide and healthy recipes to help lose weight and reverse fatty liver

NADINE SILVA

ISBN-13: 978-1717468048

ISBN-10: 1717468047

DEDICATION

To my beloved grandmother, for all her years of care and love.

TABLE OF CONTENTS

INTRODUCTION

How Important Is The Liver?

The liver is one of the most important organs in the human body, without which we cannot survive. It is often referred to as the "powerhouse" of the body. This reddish brown organ performs a couple of digestive, regulatory, excretory and immune functions.

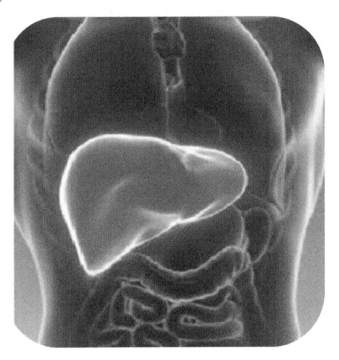

The liver is the largest internal organ having a weight of about 3 pounds in an average adult. It is located at the upper part of the abdomen mostly at the right, above the diaphragm with just a little part extending towards the left. It has several ducts and blood vessels that help in the transportation of materials to and from other parts of the body. The liver is rich in blood supply as about 13% of the total blood in the body is contained in this special organ at any point in time.

The liver is a hard working organ and carries out about 500 tasks in the body. A few important ones are highlighted below:

- Production of a digestive substance called bile which helps to break down food compounds and transport waste product.
- Getting rid of drugs and toxic substances from the blood (detoxification).
- Breaking down of fat using bile produced and aids absorption of fat in the small intestine.
- Breaking down of hemoglobin to produce bilirubin, which is used to make bile. The iron released in this process is stored in the
- bone marrow or the liver and used to make more blood cells whenever they are needed.
- Helps to breakdown carbohydrates to glucose and stores them as glycogen to be released anytime the body needs energy urgently.
- The liver helps to store minerals and vitamins such as copper, iron, vitamins K, D, B12, A and E and releases them when needed.
- It supports and aids the blood clotting process.
- Helps in the metabolism and absorption of protein compounds.
- It produces a very important blood protein called albumin which helps to transport steroid hormones and fatty acids. It also regulates the pressure of blood vessels and prevents them from leaking.
- Helps to fight infection by creating immune factors, clearing bacteria from the blood.
- Changing a harmful protein component called ammonia to urea to be excreted in the urine.

When Does A Liver Get "Fatty"?

As you can see, the liver plays several vital roles in the process of metabolism (breaking down and building up of substances in the body). These functions can be disrupted if there is excess fat in the liver. By excess

2

fat, I mean when fat covers over 5% of the liver mass. This build up of fat in the liver cells is what is referred to as fatty liver (hepatic steatosis).

A Healthy Liver

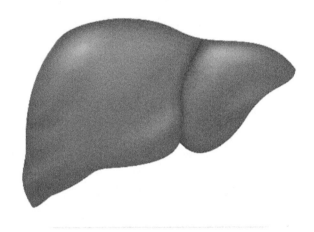

A Fatty Liver

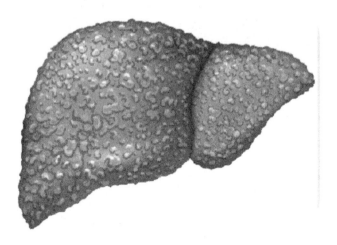

What Makes The Liver To Become "Fatty"?

First and foremost, you need to know that there are two main classification of fatty liver– alcohol induced fatty liver and non-alcohol induced fatty liver. The former, as the name implies, is caused by the constant consumption of alcohol while the later is associated with the excess deposit of fat in the liver and caused by factors not related to alcohol intake. Now let's break down these causes.

Alcohol: Everything we consume passes through the liver. However, there are some substances which are not so friendly to the liver like alcohol. Alcohol is a major enemy of the liver as it produces toxins (harmful chemicals) that directly affect the liver cells.

Diet: If fat consumed is more than what is required in the body, the liver tries to convert the excess to forms in which it can be eliminated or stored. When we eat a lot of foods with high calories like sugary foods, it limits the ability of the liver to process fats thereby resulting in the buildup of fat around the organ. Oily foods such as fried foods, if eaten in excess can also lead to the deposit of fats in the liver tissues causing a fatty liver.

Obesity: About 50% of Americans are already overweight or living with obesity. Studies show that about 75% of obese individuals are likely to develop fatty liver disease.

Medical Conditions: Fatty liver can also be caused by certain illnesses such as type II diabetes, high blood pressure, Wilson's disease, hyperlipidemia (high level of lipid in the bloodstream) and insulin resistance.

Medications: Some drugs may have adverse effect on the liver function. These medicines include aspirins, amiodarone (injection and oral), tetracycline, methotrexate, tamoxifen and steroids.

Other causes:

Rapid and excessive weight loss.

Protein malnutrition and starvation.

Genetic inheritance.

How Do You Suspect If A Person Has A Fatty Liver?

Fatty liver is a benign condition that usually has no symptom at first. So you can't know for sure if a person has a fatty liver just by looking at them. It can however develop into a condition called steatohepatitis, if not checked. Steatohepatitis simply means a fatty liver with inflammation and this can further develop into more life threatening conditions like cirrhosis (the scarring and hardening of the liver) or even cancer of the liver.

The symptoms of an inflamed fatty liver (steatohepatitis) include:

- Fatigue- general weakness and tiredness
- Upper abdominal discomfort and a feeling of fullness
- Malaise
- Confusion
- Nausea
- Appetite loss
- profuse sweating
- Easy bruising and bleeding

People with the above symptoms may not necessarily have steatohepatitis but are advised to seek medical attention for proper diagnosis.

The doctor can use several methods to detect the presence of a fatty liver. These may include:

- Investigation of medical history
- Physical examination
- Imaging studies such as ultrasound and Magnetic Resonance Imaging (MRI)
- Blood tests: to determine the presence of liver enzymes in the blood
- Biopsy of the liver.

How Do You Get Rid Of A Fatty Liver?

There is no specific medication to treat fatty liver disease. However, the condition can be reversed by undoing those things which made it occur. To remove excess liver fat, you have to focus on the gradual and sustained removal of excess body fat. This remedy can also be applied to cirrhosis and other advanced forms of inflamed fatty liver conditions. This is possible because the liver has the unique ability to regenerate and repair its damaged cells with time. Even if up to 75% of this special organ is destroyed, the liver can heal itself and grow back to its normal size if exposed to the right nutrition and conditions. Therefore, living healthy is the key to having a healthy liver.

Here are some ways to remove unwanted fats from the liver:

Regular exercise: Keep your liver fit by constant daily exercise. This will help burn the excess triglycerides in the body to release energy, reducing liver fat.

Lose weight: If you are overweight or obese, strive to lose weight by getting more active and watching what you eat (avoid large meals). Drinking a lot of water can also help you lose weight.

Eat healthy: A balanced diet can do your liver much good. Cut out food with saturated fats, high calories, added sugar and refined carbohydrates. Eat more vegetables and fruits, whole grains, high fiber plants and include proteins to every meal.

Drink responsibly: Drinking alcohol can cause the scarring of the liver. It is advised to keep off alcohol for the good of your liver but if you can't, greatly limit your alcohol intake.

Avoid non-medical drugs: A survey conducted in 2012 showed that an alarming number of Americans have used illicit substances like cocaine, marijuana, heroin, inhalants, etc. These substances are highly poisonous to the liver.

Avoid toxic chemicals: Try not to inhale cigarette smoke, aerosols like insecticides, as they may contain chemical substances that are harmful to the liver. Also reduce contact with cleaning products.

Below is a table showing the foods to include in your diet and those to avoid and cut down to maintain a healthy liver.

EAT	AVOID	CUT DOWN
Oatmeal	Alcohol	Potatoes
Walnuts	Fried food	Cereals
Sunflower seeds	Red meat	Starchy carbohydrates
Coffee	Salt	
Fatty fish: tuna, salmon, trout and sardines	Sugary foods: sodas, candies, fruit juices and cookies	Grains: corn, rye, wheat, rice, barley
Greens: spinach, broccoli, kale and Brussels sprout	Processed carbs: white bread, pasta, white rice, flour	
Tofu	Fatty meat, preserved meat	
Avocados	Margarine and butter	
Olive oil, cold pressed coconut oil	Partially hydrogenated oil	
Garlic	High fat dairy: sour cream,	
Milk		
Green tea		
Legumes		
Whole grains		
Fruits		
Nuts and seeds		
Eggs		
Cheese: cottage, feta, parmesan, pecorino and ricotta		
Unflavored yogurt		
Grape fruit		
Turmeric		

BREAKFAST RECIPES

Potato-Egg Breakfast
Start your day with a healthy potato egg breakfast.

Preparation time: 5 minutes

Cooking time: 45 minutes

Servings: 2

Ingredients:

2 eggs

¼ cup shredded hash brown potatoes, refrigerated

Directions:

1. Grease two muffin tins with cooking spray.

2. . Divide the shredded hash brown potatoes into the muffin tins.

3. Press lightly into the bottom of the cup and push up the sides of the shredded potatoes in each muffin tin just above rim. Note that the hash brown will shrink when it starts baking.

4. Bake the baskets for 30 minutes.

5. Take out the muffin cups from the oven then crack one large egg into each basket.

6. Return the muffin cup to the oven, then bake for another 12 to 15 minutes or until the eggs are cooked to your desire.

7. Once done, season with pepper and salt to taste.

Banana-Blueberry Pancake

Preparation time: 5 minutes

Cooking time: 5 minutes

Ingredients:

½ cup fresh blueberries

1½ ripe bananas

1/8 tsp baking powder

2 large eggs

Maple syrup (for serving)

Directions:

1. Peel the bananas and place them in a bowl. Mash the bananas with a potato masher or fork, making the mashed banana a little lumpy.

2. Whisk the eggs properly in another bowl, making sure the yolks are broken up and well mixed with the egg whites.

3. Pour the whisked eggs into the mashed bananas then carefully mix in the baking powder.

4. Preheat the griddle or sauté pan over medium heat, while the baking powder activates.

5. Grease the heated griddle with cooking spray then spoon 2 tbsp of the mixture onto the griddle.

6. When a lot of small bubbles appear on the surface of the pancake, place small amount of blueberries into the pancake then flip over to cook the other side of the pancake.

7. Once set, serve hot with maple syrup.

Breakfast Oatmeal

Preparation time: 2 minutes

Cooking time: 10 minutes

Servings: 1

Ingredients:

½ cup steel rolled oats, or quick oats

1 tsp ground cinnamon.

1 tsp honey

1 tsp pure maple syrup

½ cup of organic raisins

1 cup of water (boiling, if using quick oats)

Directions:

1. If using steel rolled oats: Prepare the oats according to the label directions. Note that salt is optional.

2. Once the steel rolled oats are done, add the remaining ingredients and mix very well.

3. If using quick oats: Mix all the ingredients in a bowl then add 1 cup of boiling water. Mix very well and serve.

Liver Friendly Breakfast Omelet

Preparation time: 5 minutes

Cooking time: 5 minutes

Servings: 1 or 2

Ingredients:

2 large organic eggs

Goat or feta cheese (just a little)

2 tbsp diced chives

1- 2 tbsp pesto

1/8 tsp fine grain sea salt

1/3 - ½ cup mixed salad greens

Directions:

1. In a small bowl, beat the eggs and salt with a fork. Beat thoroughly until the eggs are well mixed.

2. Heat a large non-stick skillet over medium heat then pour in the egg mixture. Swirl so that the mixture thinly spreads out across the whole pan. You may use a crepe maker or crepe pan if you like.

3. Sprinkle some chives over the eggs then let them set for about 15 seconds to 1 minute. This depends on the heat of your pan.

4. Run a spatula under the omelet then slide it out of the pan onto a large cutting board, countertop or a cookie sheet.

5. Spread the pesto on top of the omelet. If the pesto is thick, thin it a bit with water to make it spreadable.

6. Sprinkle the cheese and salad greens on top.

7. Roll the omelet from you, starting with one end. Cut it in half on a deep diagonal.

8. Season with salt if required. Garnish with a few diced chives then serve.

Creamy Chia Seed Custard

Preparation time: 5 to 10 minutes

Cooking time: 0 minute

Servings: 2

Ingredients:

6 tbsp Chia seeds

1 cup plain live yogurt

½ tsp cinnamon

¼ cup freshly squeezed orange juice

½ tsp ground sumac

2 tbsp honey

¾ cup coconut milk

½ tsp vanilla extract

Directions:

1. Pulse the chia seeds, sumac and cinnamon in a blender a few times, to get a rough powder.

2. Pour in the orange juice, yogurt, milk, honey and vanilla.

3. Pulse four to five times in two second increments. The mixture should have a consistency of a thick soup.

4. Refrigerate mixture for about 1 hour or overnight to set and provide a thicker, custard like texture.

Chinese-Style Scallion, Egg And Mushroom Omelet

Preparation time: 3 minutes

Cooking time: 5 minutes

Servings: 1

Ingredients:

2 eggs

¼ cup chopped green onion

1 tbsp low fat sour cream (or heavy cream)

1 tsp minced garlic

¼ cup chopped kale

¼ cup chopped tomato

¼ cup chopped mushroom

¼ cup diced bell pepper

Directions:

1. In a bowl, beat eggs and sour cream together until it becomes light and fluffy.

2. Heat up a small non-stick pan over medium heat. Add the onion, tomato, garlic and kale. Add the diced bell pepper and the mushroom then sauté lightly for about 2 to 3 minutes just until softened.

3. Pour in the whisked eggs then cook for about 3 minutes or until the sides of the omelet can be lifted from the pan with a spatula.

4. Flip the omelet gently then cook for another 1 minute.

5. Once done, fold the omelet in half gently then cook each sides for another 30 seconds. Serve and Enjoy!

Black Coconut Rice Pudding

Preparation time: 10 minutes

Cooking time: 30 minutes - 1 hour

Servings: 3 - 4

Ingredients:

1 cup black rice, soaked overnight

1/3 cup lightly toasted coconut flakes

1 can full-fat coconut milk

½ cup of water (for soaked rice), 1½ cups water (for unsoaked rice)

¼ tsp. fine grain sea salt

1 tbsp. maple syrup (or desired sweetener)

½ vanilla bean, optional

To serve: a few tbsp coconut milk

Directions:

1. Measure the rice, rinse then cover with water. Let it soak for up to 8 hours or overnight. Drain then rinse properly again.

2. Pour the rice into a pot. Add the coconut milk, the vanilla bean seeds with pod, salt and the indicated amount of water.

3. Bring to a boil then lower the heat to a simmer then cook covered frequently stir, until the rice becomes soft and almost all the liquid has been

absorbed. Cooking time depends on whether the rice was soaked or not. Un-soaked rice should cook for 45 to 60 minutes, while soaked rice will cook for about 25 to 30 minutes.

4. Add the maple syrup then combine by folding. Remove from heat then set it aside.

5. Prepare fruits to accompany the pudding such as mango, pomegranate, passion fruit, banana, pineapple and kiwi, while the rice is cooking.

6. To serve, spoon out desired quantity of black rice into a bowl then place the fruit on top, followed with toasted coconut then drizzle coconut milk on top. Enjoy.

Orangey-Lavender Pudding

Preparation time: 5 minutes

Cooking time: 5 minutes

Servings: 4

Ingredients:

2 oranges, peeled

1 tsp dried lavender flowers

1 cup dates

1 cup cashews

1-2 tbsp coconut oil, melted

Directions:

1. In a blender, blend all the ingredients until it turns smooth. If the consistency is too thick, thin it out with the juice of another one or two orange.

2. Spoon into small, single serving dishes just like ramekins. Refrigerate overnight.

3. On the next day, garnish the pudding with orange slices and zest, and more lavender flowers if desired. Enjoy.

Cherry-Oatmeal Pudding

Enjoy a quick and healthy breakfast of oatmeal pudding decorated with fresh yummy cherries.

Preparation time: 10 minutes

Cooking time: 10 minutes

Servings: 4

Ingredients:

1 cup dry old fashioned oats

2 cups of ripe cherries (½ cup for each serving)

2 cups unsweetened vanilla coconut milk

1 tsp ground flax seeds

3 tsp pure maple syrup

1/16 tsp sea salt (cherries)

1/16 - 1/8 ground cinnamon

Directions:

1. Combine 1½ cups of coconut milk, oats and salt in a small pot, and cook on stove-top. Stir then bring to a gentle boil. Simmer on low heat for about 8 to 10 minutes or until oats are tender and most of the liquid is absorbed.

2. Take the oats from stove then stir in the ground flax.

3. Transfer the oat to a storage bowl to cool. Now add the remaining ½ cup of milk and 2 teaspoons of maple syrup. Stir then refrigerate for at least 1 hour, but overnight will be preferable.

4. When you are ready to serve the pudding, Scoop the chilled oats into single serving bowl then top with prepared cherries.

5. To make the cherries: Wash 2 cups of fresh, ripe cherries for topping then dry.

6. Cut the cherries in half then remove the pits and stems.

7. When its 30 minutes before serving the pudding, mix the cherries, tsp of maple syrup, a dash of cinnamon and a pinch of sea salt in a small bowl. Set it aside and let it sit for 20 minutes.

8. Top the bowls of pudding with mixed cherry.

LUNCH RECIPES

Veggie-Turkey Stuffed Pepper

Preparation time: 15 minutes

Cooking time: 20 minutes

Servings: 4

Ingredients:

1 lb lean ground turkey

4 red bell peppers

2 tbsp olive oil

1 cup sliced mushrooms

½ green bell pepper, small chop

½ of onion, minced

1 zucchini, chopped

½ yellow bell pepper, small dice

1 cup fresh spinach

1 (14.5 oz.) can chopped tomatoes, drained

1 tbsp tomato paste

1 tsp Italian seasoning

½ tsp powdered garlic

Pepper and salt to taste

Directions:

1. Bring a large pot of water to a boil.

2. Cut off the tops of the peppers then take out the seeds. Cook the peppers including the tops in boiling water for 5 minutes; drain then set aside.

3. Preheat the oven to 350°F.

4. Cook the turkey in a skillet over medium heat until evenly brown then set aside.

5. Using the same pan, heat up olive oil then add the onion, zucchini, mushrooms, yellow and green bell pepper, and spinach, and cook until soft.

6. Return the turkey to the skillet and add the remaining ingredients.

7. Stuff the peppers with the mixture. Place the stuffed peppers in a sided casserole dish. Replace the tops if you like then bake for 15 minutes.

Liver Friendly Eggplant Boats

Preparation time: 10 minutes

Cooking time: 45 minutes

Servings: 1

Ingredients:

1 eggplant

2 large onions, chopped

1 red pepper, finely chopped

2 -3 tablespoons tomato paste (or ½ cup of tomato juice)

To garnish: White cheese, grated

Directions:

1. Cut the eggplant in two then place it in the oven and bake at 350°F. Let it cook for about 30 minutes.

2. While the eggplant is cooking, prepare the filling: Chop the onions and brown them in water (this can be done by adding just a little water first, then keep stirring and add more water as needed).

3. Chop the red pepper finely then add it close to the onions, cook for about 5 minutes or more, or when they are properly cooked.

4. Add ½ cup of tomato juice or two spoons of tomato paste. Let the flavor combine for about 2 minutes.

5. Take out the cooked eggplants from the oven with a spoon, ensuring the jacket is unbroken.

6. Mix the eggplant with the onions and peppers then spoon the mixture back into the eggplant.

7. Top with grated cheese then bake in the oven at 400°F for 10 minutes. Enjoy.

Healthy Bulgur Tabbouleh

Preparation time: 15 minutes

Cooking time: 10 minutes

Servings: 2

Ingredients:

2/3 cup cracked wheat (medium-fine bulgur)

1 cup vegetable stock

1 large tomato, seeds removed and chopped

1 serrano pepper, seeds removed and chopped

1 tsp grated fresh ginger

1 bell pepper, seeds removed and chopped

1 tsp ancho chili powder

½ cup fresh cilantro, diced

½ cup fresh mint, diced

1 tsp olive oil

2 limes, zest grated and juiced

Directions:

1. Put the stock in a pot and bring to boil.

2. Place bulgur in a small sauce pan with lid. Pour the broth over the bulgur.

3. Cover the pan and let the bulgur absorb the liquid for about 15 minutes.

4. Drain excess broth then fluff with a fork.

5. While the bulgur/wheat cools, toss the veggies, herbs and spices together with oil and lime juice then let it marinate for 5 minutes.

6. Add the bulgur then serve chilled.

7. You can serve in halved bell peppers.

Spiced Chickpea 'N' Sautéed Artichoke

Preparation time: 5 minutes

Cooking time: 5 - 7 minutes

Servings: 4

Ingredients:

1½ cup cooked chickpeas, rinsed

2 tsp turmeric

1½ cup artichoke hearts, rinsed

3 tbsp extra virgin olive oil

½ tsp cracked black pepper

½ tsp sea salt

1 tbsp minced garlic

1 tsp coriander (optional)

1 tsp ginger (optional)

Directions:

1. Heat a large cast iron skillet or sauté pan over medium-high heat.

2. In a bowl, mix the chickpeas, olive oil, artichoke hearts and seasonings together until well coated.

3. Once the pan is hot, toss all the ingredients into the pan then shake to prevent it from sticking to the pan.

4. Stir the mixture once a minute then cook for 5 to 6 minutes or until the chickpeas have a nice brown crust.

5. Squeeze in lemon juice over the sauté and serve at once. Serve with whole wheat pita bread or refrigerate for later. The mixture will hold for up to three days in fridge. Enjoy!

Veggie Wrap With Sunflower Seed Spread

Prepare a power lunch of veggie detox wrap with sunflower seed spread. Enjoy!

Preparation time: 15 minutes

Cooking time: 15 minutes

Servings: 2 wraps

Ingredients:

For Sunflower Seed Spread:

1 cup of sunflower seeds, soaked overnight

2 to 3 sundried tomatoes

1 large tomato

¼ bunch cilantro

3 tbsp extra virgin olive oil

2 tbsp tahini

2 lemons, juiced

¼ tbsp sea salt

¼ tbsp black pepper

Optional wrap toppings:

¼ cup cultured veggies

Shredded carrots

Sprouts

Sliced peppers, red cabbage, etc

Directions:

1. To make the sunflower seed spread: Drain water from the sunflower seeds then place the seeds in a blender or food processor. Add the rest of the ingredients, and blend until it becomes smooth.

2. Add 1 to 2 tbsp of water if required, to achieve desired consistency.

3. To arrange the wrap, scoop 2 to 3 tbsp of the spread to your chosen wrap. Add preferred toppings then roll it up. Enjoy.

Tuna 'N' Cabbage-Corn Fritters

Preparation time: 15 minutes

Cooking time: 20 minutes

Servings: 20 fritters

Ingredients:

1 (4-5 oz.) canned tuna in spring water, drained

¼ cabbage, thinly shredded

1 (14.75 oz) tin creamed corn

1 small onion, finely chopped

1/3 cup self raising flour

2 eggs, lightly whisked

¼ cup reduced fat milk

Olive oil spray

Directions:

1. Combine all the ingredients in a large bowl, mix properly then let it stand for 10 minutes

2. Heat up a non-stick fry pan over a medium heat then grease with oil spray.

3. Spoon tablespoons of the mixture into the heated frying pan

4. Fry both sides until golden.

5. Serve with sweet chili sauce

6. To get a smoother consistency, blend the mixture in a blender before frying.

Note: it can be stored in the fridge and suitable for freezing

Broccoli - Shrimpy Stir Fry

Preparation time: 10 minutes

Cooking time: 20 minutes

Servings: 2

Ingredients:

8 oz peeled shrimp

1 head broccoli, sliced into small florets and steamed lightly

1 large handful of roasted cashews

2 tbsp olive oil, macadamia nut oil or duck fat

3 tbsp coconut aminos

1 tbsp fish sauce

½ red bell pepper, sliced

2 garlic cloves, crushed

2 tbsp lime juice

1 tbsp sesame seeds

Pepper and salt, to taste

Directions:

1. Heat up oil or duck fat in a wok or frying pan. Add the red pepper, garlic, cashews and sesame seeds.

2. Add the shrimp then stir fry for some minutes, until almost cooked. Add the broccoli.

3. In a bowl, combine coconut aminos, fish sauce, lime juice, pepper and salt then whisk together. Pour the mixture into the frying pan and cook

Mashed Garlicky Sweet Potatoes

Preparation time: 5 minutes

Cooking time: 10 minutes

Servings: 4

Ingredients:

3 lbs peeled sweet potatoes (cooked until soft)

1 tbsp extra virgin olive oil

1/3 cup Greek yogurt

½ brown onion, diced finely

2 tsp dried oregano

2 cloves of garlic, grated

Pepper

Salt, to taste

Directions:

1. Cook the potatoes, while its cooking, sauté the onion and garlic in the olive oil for about 8 to 10 minutes or until aromatic and translucent.

2. In a large bowl, mix all the ingredients then mash until smooth.

3. Serve with seafood, red meat or poultry.

Liver Friendly Veggie Quinoa Pilaf

Preparation time: 10 minutes

Cooking time: 20 minutes

Servings: 4

Ingredients:

2 cups quinoa

4 cups veggie stock

2 tbsp olive oil

1 medium red and yellow pepper each, diced

1 small head of broccoli, diced

6 cherry tomatoes, sliced in halves

2 medium zucchinis, diced

2 large carrots, sliced thinly

1 cup of diced pumpkin

1 brown onion, diced

1 tbsp dried oregano

1 tsp of cumin, ground

2 tbsp tomato paste

Pepper

Salt, to taste

Directions:

1. Rinse the quinoa then cook in a large pot containing veggie stock for about 15 minutes, or until it becomes soft.

2. Pour olive oil into a large pot then heat over medium heat. Add onion and sauté for about 3 minutes, or until tender.

3. Add the remaining ingredients except the quinoa.

4. Stir then gently cooks until the veggies have softened. Add some water if the veggies are sticking to the base of the pot.

5. Once cooked, add the veggie mixture to the quinoa mixture. Stir properly and serve.

DINNERS RECIPES

Easy Delicious Hummus

Preparation time: 10 minutes

Cooking time: 1 hour

Servings: 2

Ingredients:

1 cup of chickpeas

½ tsp pepper flakes or paprika

½ - 1 tsp salt

4 tbsp tahini

2 garlic cloves

½ lemon, juice

Water

Directions:

1. Soak the chickpeas in 4 cups of water for 12 hours or overnight. Discard the water then rinse the chickpeas and transfer to a large pot. Cover with about 8 to 9 cups of water.

2. Bring to a boil, then lower heat to low and simmer for 1 hour or until they are well cooked. Add more water if required then stir occasionally.

3. Once done, drain the chickpeas then transfer to a blender. Add ½ cup of the cooking water then add another half if required.

4. Process the chickpeas then add salt to taste. Add tahini, lemon juice, garlic cloves and pepper flakes or paprika. Add more pepper flakes for extra flavor. Pulse again until you achieve a creamy hummus.

5. Transfer hummus to a bowl and enjoy. You may sprinkle some extra paprika on top. Don't add extra oil because tahini contains enough fat.

Veggie-Chicken Skillet

Preparation time: 10 minutes

Cooking time: 30 minutes

Servings: 2

Ingredients:

1 tsp oil

½ lb chicken, sliced into strips

1 small onion, chopped

½ cup minced carrots

1 sliced zucchini

½ bell pepper, chopped

2 tbsp water

Directions:

1. Pour oil into a skillet then add the chicken strips and cook all sides until well browned and the juices are cleared.

2. Transfer the chicken to a bowl to keep warm.

3. In the same skillet, add the onion, carrots, pepper and zucchini, and then cook for 5 to 10 minutes, until the veggies become tender. You can add more liquid (2 tbsp of water) if there isn't enough liquid there.

4. Once the veggies are cooked, add the chicken, add salt then stir everything together for a minute before serving.

Healthy Spinach Quesadillas

Preparation time: 10 minutes

Cooking time: 30 minutes

Servings: 4 - 6

Ingredients:

4 cups spinach

1 onion (or 4 green onions), chopped

1 large tomato, chopped

½ lemon juice

1 tsp cumin

Powdered garlic

Salt (optional)

1 cup shredded cheese

Directions:

1. In a skillet, cook the spinach, green onions, tomato, cumin and lemon juice. Add a little bit of powdered garlic and salt.

2. Cook then stir until the spinach is wilted then transfer to a bowl. Add 1 cup of shredded cheese (or preferred choice).

3. This is enough to fill 4 to 6 tortillas. Place the spinach-cheese mixture on half of the tortilla then fold the other half over.

4. Cook each side for 2 minutes on a griddle. Serve them hot!

Veggie 'N' Garlicky Salmon

Preparation time: 10 minutes

Cooking time: 20 minutes

Servings: 2

Ingredients:

2 lb salmon fillet

2 tbsp chopped parsley

4 cloves of garlic, minced

½ tsp salt

2 tbsp water

Directions:

1. Put the salmon on a baking sheet, on a baking tray.

2. Combine the parsley, salt, garlic and water, and then rub the mixture all over the salmon.

3. Preheat the oven to 400°F then cover the tray with an aluminum foil or cap. Cook for 15 to 20 minutes or until ready.

4. You can remove the cover after 10 to 15 minutes and then let the salmon cook for another 5 minutes if you want it darker and crispier.

5. Serve with veggies.

Herby Mushroom Rice Casserole

Preparation time: 5 minutes

Cooking time: 35 minutes

Servings: 3

Ingredients:

4 cups diced mushrooms

5 scallions, chopped (both green and white parts)

2 cups cooked brown rice

2 tbsp unsalted butter

1 tsp minced garlic

½ tsp cayenne pepper

½ tsp ground black pepper

1 tsp dried oregano

1 small bunch of fresh parsley (remove stems and mince)

2 medium bunches dill (remove stems and mince)

1½ cup veggie stock

Directions:

1. Melt butter in a large skillet over medium heat.

2. Cook the scallion and garlic, stirring for about 5 minutes or until the onions are translucent.

3. Add the cayenne, pepper and oregano, then cook for another 1 minute.

4. Add the mushroom, parsley, and dill, and cook for about 5 to 10 minutes or until the mushrooms are tender.

5. Preheat the oven to 350°F.

6. In a 2½ quart casserole dish, combine the rice with the veggie mixture.

7. Pour the veggie stock over the entire dish and bake for 30 minutes, uncovered.

Shallot - Ginger Spiced Red Snapper

Preparation time: 10 minutes

Cooking time: 8 to 10 minutes

Servings: 4

Ingredients:

1½ lbs. red snapper (washed, dried and sliced into 2" pieces)

8 shallots, minced

2 tsp turmeric

½ tsp sea salt flakes, divided

2 tbsp finely chopped garlic

2 tbsp finely chopped ginger

1 dried red chili, crumbled

2 tbsp peanut oil

2 limes, halved for squeezing

Salmon or halibut (or desired fish)

Directions:

1. Toss the fish in turmeric then set aside.

2. Grind the shallots and half of the sea salt into a paste with a mortar and pestle. Transfer to another bowl.

3. Grind the remaining salt, ginger and garlic in the empty mortar.

4. Heat up a large skillet to medium.

5. Add ½ tbsp of peanut oil and the shallot paste then cook until a bit browned, about 5 minutes.

6. Add the chili and ginger-garlic mixture and then cook for another 5 minutes.

7. Add the remaining oil then add the fish then cook for 1½ to 2 minutes.

8. Flip over the pieces then cook for another 1½ to 2 minutes, depending on your desired doneness.

9. Turn off the heat then squeeze fresh lime juice over the whole dish.

10. Serve with brown rice.

Healthy Garlic Spiced Chicken

Preparation time: 10 minutes

Cooking time: 40 minutes

Servings: 4

Ingredients:

3 lbs. chicken drumsticks

1 tbsp smoked paprika

¼ cup olive oil

1 tbsp powdered garlic

1 tbsp ground cumin

½ tsp powdered chili, or more

½ tsp salt

Directions:

1. In a large bowl, combine all the ingredients except the chicken. Now, add the chicken drumsticks then coat with your hands until well combined.

2. Cook the chicken on both sides on a barbecue over medium heat for about 20 minutes or until well cooked.

3. Serve with a salad.

Veggies 'N' Buckwheat Noodles

Prepare a healthy dinner of vegetables and buckwheat noodles. This simple meal is relaxing for the liver.

Preparation time: 5 minutes

Cooking time: 6 minutes

Servings: 4 to 6

Ingredients:

8 oz. (1 pack) buckwheat noodles

1 cup thinly sliced or shredded carrots

1 tsp brown rice vinegar

1 cup peas

1½ cups snow peas, sliced

1 tbsp fresh ginger root, grated

1 tbsp toasted sesame oil

1 tbsp tamari

1 scallion, finely diced (only the green part)

1 tbsp black sesame seeds

Directions:

1. Cook the buckwheat noodles according to the cooking instructions on the wrapper. When it's a minute before the noodles are ready, add the veggies, and finish cooking.

2. Drain the buckwheat noodles then set aside. If you are preparing ahead of time, stop the cooking process with cold water.

3. Warm up the sesame oil and ginger then cook for a minute.

4. Add the noodles, vinegar and tamari, and then toss properly. Garnish with scallion and sesame seeds. Serve.

Healthy Chicken Salsa

Preparation time: 10 minutes

Cooking time: 30 minutes

Servings: 2 to 4

Ingredients:

1 lb. chicken breast, skin and bone removed, slice into 1" pieces

Olive oil

1 large onion, diced

1 large green/red pepper, diced

2 tomatoes, diced

3 cloves of garlic, minced

1 can of kidney beans, rinsed and drained

1 bunch of broccoli

1 cup medium salsa

Fresh cilantro

Pepper and salt

Directions:

1. Heat up 1 tbsp of olive oil in a large non stick skillet.

2. Add onion and garlic, sauté for about 3 minutes or until they become tender. Add the pepper then sauté again for 2 minutes.

3. Now, add the remaining ingredients then bring the mixture to a boil. Lower the heat, cover and simmer for 5 minutes, or until the chicken is well cooked.

4. Serve with mashed potatoes, rice or noodles.

SNACKS RECIPES

Homemade Gingersnaps

Preparation time: 30 minutes

Cooking time: 10 minutes

Servings: 18 gingersnaps

Ingredients:

1¾ cups white whole wheat flour

1 tsp baking powder

1½ tsp cornstarch

1¾ tsp ground ginger

1/8 tsp of ground nutmeg

¼ tsp ground cinnamon

1/8 tsp of ground cloves

1 large egg white, room temperature

¼ tsp salt

2 tbsp of unsalted butter, melted

2¼ tsp of vanilla stevia

2 tsp vanilla extract

¼ cup molasses

¼ cup of nonfat milk, at room temperature

3 tbsp of granulated sweetener (or as required)

Directions:

1. Preheat the oven to 325°F. Line a baking sheet with a parchment paper.

2. Whisk the flour, baking powder, cornstarch, cinnamon, ginger, cloves, nutmeg and salt together in a medium bowl.

3. In another bowl, whisk the egg, butter, vanilla extract and stevia together. Stir in the milk and molasses, and then add the flour mixture, stirring until well combined.

4. Divide the dough into 18 equal sizes then roll each portion into a ball. Working with one ball at a time, roll in the granulated sweetener until well coated.

5. Place the coated balls on the prepared baking sheet. Use the flat bottom of a drinking glass to flatten to desired width. Note that these cookies do not spread while baking.

6. Sprinkle more granulated sweetener over the flattened cookie dough, then press it down gently into the cookie dough with your fingertips.

7. Place in the oven and bake for 8 to 10 minutes at 325°F. Once ready, let it cool on the baking sheet for 10 minutes before transferring them to a wire rack.

Buttery Rice Krispie

Preparation time: 5 minutes

Cooking time: 5 minutes

Servings: 16 bars

Ingredients:

4 cups of gluten free puffed brown rice cereal

2/3 cup honey

½ cup peanut butter

1 tsp vanilla extract

1/16 tsp salt

Directions:

1. Combine all the ingredients in medium sized mixing bowl, ensuring they incorporate.

2. Transfer the mixture to a parchment paper lined 8 by 8 square baking pan.

3. Spread the mixture across the pan then push down gently into the pan and its corners.

4. Refrigerate for 1 hour to set.

5. Take out then slice into 16 bars and enjoy!

6. The bars can be refrigerated or kept in the freezer for up to 1 month.

Cooking tip: Use a peanut butter that has only peanuts as its listed ingredient.

Apple-Oatmeal Cookies

Preparation time: 5 minutes (+ 30 minutes rest time)

Cooking time: 13 to 15 minutes

Servings: 15 Cookies

Ingredients:

1 medium sized red apple (or 1 cup if finely chopped)

1 cup instant oats

1½ tsp baking powder

¾ cup whole wheat flour

1½ tsp ground cinnamon

2 tbsp unsalted butter or coconut oil, melted

1/8 tsp salt

½ cup pure maple syrup or honey

1 large egg, room temperature

1 tsp vanilla extract

Directions:

1. In a large bowl, mix flour, baking powder, oats, salt, and cinnamon together.

2. In another bowl, whisk butter or coconut oil, egg and vanilla together. Once combined, stir in the maple syrup or honey.

3. Pour the butter-egg mixture into the flour mixture, stirring until well mixed. Note that over-stirring can lead to tough cookies.

4. Fold in the apple then refrigerate for 30 minutes.

5. Once the dough is chilled, preheat the oven to 325°F.

6. Spoon about 2 tbsp of the cookie dough and drop into 15 evenly rounded scoops onto the baking sheet lined with parchment, then slightly flatten.

7. Bake for 13 to 15 minutes at 325°F. Once ready, let it cool on the pan for 10 minutes before transferring to a wire rack.

Quinoa Meat Tacos

Ditch ground beef for a healthy liver friendly taco meat made with quinoa. Its flavorful, hot and crispy.

Preparation time: 15 minutes

Cooking time: 45 minutes

Servings: 3½ cups

Ingredients:

1 cup quinoa

¾ cup water

1 cup veggie broth

1 tbsp avocado or olive oil

½ cup salsa (a bit chunky)

2 tsp ground cumin

2 tsp ground powdered chili

1 tbsp nutritional yeast

½ tsp powdered garlic

½ tsp black pepper

½ tsp sea salt

Directions:

1. Heat up a medium saucepan over medium heat. When heated, add the rinsed quinoa then toast for 4 to 5 minutes, stirring consistently.

2. Pour in the veggie broth and water then bring to a boil over medium-high heat. Lower the heat to low then cover with its lid.

3. Cook for about 15 to 25 minutes, or until the liquid is completely absorbed. With a fork, fluff then open lid. Remove from heat then let it rest for 10 minutes.

4. Preheat the oven to 375°F.

5. In a large mixing bowl, add the cooked quinoa then add the remaining ingredients; salsa, cumin, nutritional yeast, powdered garlic, powdered chili, oil, pepper and salt.

6. Toss to properly combine. Now, spread the mixture on a lightly sprayed or parchment lined baking sheet.

7. Bake for 20 to 35 minutes, tossing/stirring once when its halfway through cooking time to make sure it is evenly baking. Once the quinoa is ready, it will be golden brown and fragrant. Be careful so you don't burn yourself!

8. Serve in soft or crispy taco shells. Serve with taco salads, nachos, tostadas, or in enchiladas.

9. Leftovers can be refrigerated for up to 4 to 5 days. Reheat in a skillet on the stovetop or in the microwave or in an oven at 350°F.

Cooking tip: Veggie broth gives extra flavor to the quinoa but you can substitute with water then adjust salsa/spices as required.

Honey Coconut-Cashew Cookie

Preparation time: 5 to 10 minutes

Cooking time: 20 to 25 minutes

Servings: 24 small cookies

Ingredients:

½ cup natural honey

½ cup finely ground cashews

½ cup coconut oil

½ cup almond flour

1 tbsp lecithin

1 cup unsweetened shredded coconut

1 cup rolled oats

¼ whole wheat flour (or extra almond flour for gluten-free)

½ tsp salt

¼ cup almond or coconut milk

Directions:

1. Preheat the oven to 350°F.

2. Mix the honey, coconut oil, almond flour, lecithin and ground cashews together until creamy.

3. Add the shredded coconut, whole wheat flour, oats and salt, then mix to combine.

4. Pour in the milk then stir until smooth.

5. Using two spoons, scoop and drop the cookie dough on a baking sheet lined with parchment, about 2" apart.

6. This mix will make about 24 medium-sized cookies.

7. Bake for 20 to 25 minutes, check towards the end of cooking for doneness.

8. Adjust cooking time depending on your desired size. Once cooled, the cookies will be hard so remove them from the oven when they are still slightly soft to the touch in the middle.

Italian-Style Quinoa Bites

Preparation time: 5 to 7 minutes

Cooking time: 20 minutes

Servings: 24 mini muffins

Ingredients:

1 cup of cooked quinoa

½ cup shredded zucchini

2 large eggs

1 egg white

½ cup finely diced sun-dried tomatoes

2 tbsp parsley, diced

2 tbsp green onions, diced

½ cup of grated cheese

1 tbsp diced basil

Sea salt to taste

Black pepper to taste

Directions:

1. Preheat the oven to 350°F.

2. In a large bowl, combine all the ingredients then completely mix.

3. Lightly spray a mini muffin pan then equally spoon the mixture into the muffin wells.

4. Bake for 15 to 20 minutes, until they are golden brown. (Bake for 25 to 30 minutes if using a regular-sized muffin pan).

5. Take out then let them cool for 10 minutes.

6. Detach the edges with a paring knife if the mini muffin are sticking.

7. If you want to freeze, arrange the muffins in a single layer on a baking sheet then completely freeze before you transfer to a freezer bag.

Cheesy Smoked Salmon Rolls

Preparation time: 20 minutes

Cooking time: 0 minute

Servings: 8

Ingredients:

8 pieces of smoked salmon

16 water cracker biscuits

3.5 oz. low-fat ricotta cheese

2 oz. extra light cream cheese

1 tsp capers

1 tsp lemon juice

¼ tsp lemon zest

1 tsp chives or spring onions, diced

1 tsp dill, diced

Directions:

1. Place the salmon on a clean board.

2. Combine all the remaining ingredients except the biscuits in a bowl then mix well.

3. Spread 1 tbsp of the mixture over each piece of salmon.

4. Roll up the salmon into a tube.

5. Serve with water crackers.

Cooking tip: The salmon rolls can also be sliced up and placed onto the water crackers. Store leftover in a plastic bag in the fridge. It is not freezer friendly.

Protein Gingerbread Balls

Preparation time: 10 minutes

Cooking time: 0 minute

Servings: 12 balls

Ingredients:

1 tbsp ground ginger

1 cup roasted almonds

1 cup roasted walnuts

½ cup unsweetened coconut flakes

1 tsp ground cloves

1 tbsp chia seeds

2 tbsp honey

Directions:

1. Combine all the ingredients in a blender then pulse until well ground and the mixture incorporates. Add a little water if the mixture is a bit dry.

2. Mold the mixture into balls then store in an airtight container in the fridge.

Sweet Coconut Morsels

This is the perfect sugar free snack for fatty liver and quite handy when getting a sugar craving.

Preparation time: 20 minutes

Cooking time: 0 minute

Servings: 12 to 24

Ingredients:

1 cup unsweetened shredded coconut

2 tbsp coconut oil

2 cups raw cashews

¼ cup fresh lime juice

Directions:

1. Pour the cashews into a blender then process until you get a fine meal.

2. Add all the remaining ingredients then pulse until smooth. Add a little more or less lime juice if required. This depends on the size of the coconut and the moisture in the nuts.

3. Mold the mixture into balls then store in an airtight container in the fridge.

SOUPS RECIPES

Healthy Tuscan Veggie Soup

Preparation time: 20 minutes

Cooking time: 35 minutes

Servings: 6 servings

Ingredients:

1 (15 oz.) can reduced-sodium cannellini beans, drained and rinsed

2 carrots, chopped (about ½ cup)

1 tbsp olive oil

½ large onion, chopped (about 1 cup)

2 stalks celery, chopped (about ½ cup)

1 small zucchini, chopped (about 1½ cups)

1 garlic clove, minced

1 tbsp diced fresh thyme leaves (or 1 tsp dried)

2 tsp diced fresh sage leaves (or ½ tsp dried)

½ tsp salt

¼ tsp freshly ground black pepper

32 oz. reduced-sodium veggie or chicken broth

14.5 oz. (1 can) no-salt-added chopped tomatoes

2 cups diced baby spinach leaves

1/3 cup freshly grated Parmesan, (optional)

Directions:

1. Mash half of the beans with the back of a spoon or masher in a small bowl then set aside.

2. Heat up oil in a large soup pot over medium-high heat. Add the onion, celery, carrots, garlic, zucchini, sage, thyme, pepper and salt, and then cook for about 5 minutes, stirring occasionally until the veggies are tender.

3. Pour in the broth and tomatoes including the juice, and then bring to a boil. Add the whole and mashed beans, the spinach leaves, and then cook for about 3 minutes or until the spinach is wilted.

4. Garnish with Parmesan, if desired. Serve.

Arugula-Broccoli Soup

Preparation time: 3 minutes

Cooking time: 20 minutes

Servings: 2

Ingredients:

1 (2/3 lb) head broccoli, sliced into small florets

1 tbsp olive oil

1 clove of garlic, diced

½ yellow onion, coarsely chopped

2½ cups veggie stock or water

¼ tsp salt

¼ tsp freshly ground black pepper

¼ tsp dried thyme

1 cup arugula leaves, packed

½ lemon juice

Directions:

1. Heat oil in a large saucepan over medium heat.

2. Add the onion then cook until tender and translucent.

3. Add the garlic then cook for 1 minute.

4. Add the broccoli then cook for 4 minutes until it turns bright green.

5. Add veggie stock or water, pepper, thyme and salt.

6. Bring to a boil, then cover and reduce heat. Cook for about 8 minutes until the broccoli is soft.

7. Pour the soup carefully into the blender or use an immersion blender. Add the arugula and blend until smooth.

8. When using the blender, start slowly and be careful. Place the cover on top of the blender but do not press down the lid. Work in batches if necessary.

9. Add the lemon juice then serve.

Liver Friendly Minestrone Soup

Preparation time: 10 minutes

Cooking time: 45 minutes

Servings: 6

Ingredients:

1 cup of green beans (sliced into ½" pieces)

2 large onions, diced

2 cups diced celery

2 cloves of garlic, minced

3 large carrots, chopped

1½ cups of dried kidney beans

1 large bell pepper, chopped

1 cup frozen peas

1 can diced tomatoes

2 cups tomato sauce

2 tbsp fresh basil (or 1 tsp dried)

Salt to taste

6 cups water

For topping; 1 tbsp grated Parmesan cheese

Directions:

1. Pour 6 cups of water into a large stock pot, add the onions, celery and carrots, and boil at medium heat.

2. Once the water starts to boil, add the green beans, frozen peas, bell pepper and chopped tomatoes. Let the soup boil for about 30 minutes then add extra water if required. The soup should be thick, but not too thick.

3. After 30 minutes, add the basil and tomato sauce then add salt to taste. Let it simmer for 5 to 10 minutes then add the garlic. Simmer for another 5 minutes or longer if the veggies are not cooked.

4. When serving, top the soup with Parmesan cheese. Enjoy!

Veggie-Potato Soup

Preparation time: 10 minutes

Cooking time: 10 minutes

Servings: 6

Ingredients:

1 small ripe peeled butternut pumpkin, chopped

1 large peeled carrot, chopped

1 large peeled potato, chopped

1 large onion, diced

2 large cloves of garlic, sliced

34 oz. salt-reduced chicken stock

1 veggie stock cube (dissolved in 1 tbsp of hot water)

1 tsp curry powder or paste

Black pepper to taste

2 tbsp light cream (optional)

1 tbsp olive oil

Directions:

1. Gently fry the onion in olive oil in a large pan. Add the sliced garlic then cook until soft

2. Add the curry powder/paste then cook for 1 minute

3. Add all the prepared veggies and the chicken stock, and then bring to a boil

4. Reduce the heat, cover with the pan then gently simmer until the veggies are soft.

5. Transfer soup to a blender then blend. Season with black pepper then add the cream (if desired).

Note: Use a ripe pumpkin not fibrous. You can buy 2, cut in halves so you can see the pumpkin

Tasty Beans - Veggie Soup

Preparation time: 15 minutes

Cooking time: 25 minutes

Servings: 6

Ingredients:

1 tbsp oil

1 onion, chopped

1 fresh clove of garlic, minced (or 1 tsp)

1 tsp cumin

1 red and green capsicum each, diced

2 large carrots, diced

14 oz. can of crushed tomatoes

51 oz. low-salt beef stock

½ cup brown or red lentils

1 zucchini, diced

1 small sweet potato, chopped

14oz. tin red kidney beans, drained and rinsed

Directions:

1. In a large pan, heat oil over medium heat. Add onion, cumin and garlic then cook until the onion becomes soft.

2. Add the stock, carrots, tomatoes, zucchini, lentils and capsicum, and then bring to a boil.

3. Lower the heat then simmer for about 20 minutes.

4. Add the kidney beans then simmer for some minutes.

6. Pour the soup into a blender then puree, or serve as it is.

Note: The soup can be stored covered in the fridge and its suitable for freezing.

Creamy Broccoli-Leek Soup

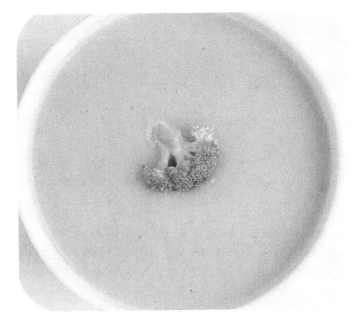

Preparation time: 10 minutes

Cooking time: 25

Servings: 4

Ingredients:

Olive oil spray

1 leek (the pale part only, cut in halve lengthwise then thinly sliced)

2 thick slices of whole meal bread (remove crusts then slice into ½" pieces)

2 cloves of garlic, minced

1 large peeled potato, finely diced

4 cups water

1 low-salt veggie stock cube, crumbled

21 oz. broccoli cut into florets

¼ cup fresh basil leaves

¼ cup fresh parsley leaves

¼ cup reduced-fat sour cream

Directions:

1. Preheat the oven to392°F. Put the bread on a baking tray then lightly spray with olive oil spray. Bake for 10 minutes or until golden, turning once.

2. While the bread is baking, heat up a large saucepan over medium heat. Grease with olive oil spray then add the leek. Cook until tender, occasionally stirring, about 5 minutes. Add the garlic then cook for 30 seconds or until fragrant.

3. Add the potato, stock cube and water to the leek mixture then bring to a boil. Lower the heat to low then simmer for 10 minutes.

4. Add the broccoli then simmer for 5 minutes or until it becomes tender. Set aside to slightly cool.

5. Pour the broccoli mixture, basil and parsley into the blender then blend until smooth. Pour the soup into a clean saucepan and cook over medium-low heat, stirring until it heats through.

6. Scoop soup into serving bowls then top with croutons and sour cream. Season with pepper and serve.

Note: The soup can be stored covered in glad-wrap in the fridge. This soup is not suitable for freezing.

Hot Broccoli - Sweet Potato Curry

This curry is so yummy and easy to make.

Preparation time: 15 minutes

Cooking time: 20 minutes

Servings: 4

Ingredients:

2 sweet potatoes

1 head broccoli (about 1 lb)

2 cloves of garlic

1 (1" piece) fresh ginger

1 - 3 fresh hot chilies

4 green onions

2 tbsp canola oil

½ tsp fine sea salt

2 (15 oz.) cans coconut milk

 Garnish: cilantro (optional)

Directions:

1. Trim the broccoli then slice into small-size florets. Peel the broccoli stem then slice into thin rounds. Peel the sweet potatoes then slice them into small-size pieces.

2. Peel the garlic and mince. Chop the chilies finely; trim the green onions and slice. Peel the ginger and grate. Set them all aside.

3. Heat up oil in a medium sized pot over high heat. Add the onions, garlic, ginger, chilies and salt. Cook for about 30 second, stirring, until sizzling and

aromatic. Add the sweet potatoes and pour in the coconut milk, then bring to the boil. Lower heat to a simmer then cook for 10 minutes.

4. Add the broccoli and cook for about 10 minutes or until the veggies are soft.

5. Serve hot over cooked rice and top with cilantro, if you desire.

Cooking tip: This curry is best made with regular coconut milk because it has a lot of flavor and it keeps the curry together even when boiled. If you decide to use low-fat coconut milk, don't let the curry come to the boil or else it will separate.

Soba Noodles In Mushroom Broth

This broth is light, warming and packed with nutrients that would do the liver a lot of good.

Preparation time: 10 minutes

Cooking time: 15 minutes

Servings: 4

Ingredients:

3 oz. maitake mushrooms, sliced (or 1 oz. dried shiitake mushrooms, soaked in warm water for 30 minutes) throw away the stems and thinly slice, about 1¼ cup.

2 tbsp sesame oil

2 large shallots, chopped finely (½ cup)

4 cloves of garlic, finely diced

1 tbsp peeled fresh ginger root, finely diced

4 cups mushroom broth

2 cups water (or water used for soaking the mushrooms if using shiitakes)

1 pack of soba noodles

1 medium-sized peeled carrot, sliced on the bias

1 cup scallions, diced

2 tbsp tamari, or to taste

½ cup of cilantro leaves (for garnish)

Lime wedges (optional)

Directions:

1. In a large pot, heat oil over medium heat.

2. Add the shallots, ginger, garlic and maitake, then sauté for 3 to 4 minutes.

3. Add the dash and 2 cups of water, then bring to the boil.

4. Add the soba noodles, stir, and then bring to the boil again.

5. Lower the heat then simmer for 5 minutes.

6. Add the carrots then simmer for 2 minutes.

7. Stir in tamari and the scallions.

8. Serve at once, top with cilantro leaves and lime wedges if you like. The lime will add a touch of brightness to this delicious soup.

Spanish-Style Celery - Rice Soup

Preparation time: 10 minutes

Cooking time: 50 minutes

Servings: 4

Ingredients:

¾ cup raw brown rice

2 cups celery, diced

1 green/ red bell pepper, diced

2 carrots, sliced

1 onion, diced

2 tomatoes, pureed

2 cloves of garlic, diced

2 tsp ground cumin

Mild green chilies, diced

1 tsp powdered chili

2 tbsp of paprika

Directions:

1. Pour water into a large pot and bring to a boil.

2. Add the rice, onion, carrots, garlic, celery and 1 tbsp of paprika, and continue to boil. Cover the pot then lower the heat and simmer about 30 minutes. Add more water if required.

3. Now, add the rest of the ingredients then simmer for 15 to 20 minutes or until the rice is soft. You have a healthy and delicious rice soup. Serve immediately.

SALAD RECIPES

Sweet Paprika Cucumber Salad

Preparation time: 2 hrs 5 minutes

Cooking time: 0 minute

Servings: 8

Ingredients:

2 English cucumbers

1 tsp sweet Hungarian paprika

½ of onion

2 tbsp seasoned salt

½ cup white vinegar

2 tsp sugar

¼ cup water

1 tbsp sour cream (optional)

1/8 tsp dried or fresh dill (optional)

Directions:

1. Peel the cucumbers then slice very thinly with a mandolin.

2. Set the cucumber slices on a large baking sheet then sprinkle salt all over, making sure that all the slices are salted. Let it sit for 30 minutes. By now, the salt will pull out the moisture from the cucumbers.

3. Slice the onion very thinly then place in a bowl.

4. Wait for the cucumbers to release water then squeeze out excess liquid with your hands. The liquid released will rinse out the salt but you may

choose to rinse the cucumber slices completely in a colander and then squeeze out excess liquid.

5. The cucumbers are supposed to be limp, yet crisp. Add the cucumbers to the onions.

6. Pour in the vinegar, sugar, water and paprika.

7. Let the cucumbers-onions mixture marinate in the refrigerator for at least 1½ hours.

8. Take out the marinated cucumbers from the fridge, add dill (if you like), and serve.

9. If you want to use the optional sour cream, discard some of the liquid after the cucumbers and onions have been marinated and then mix in the sour cream.

Healthy Potato Salad

Preparation time: 3 minutes

Cooking time: 10 - 15 minutes

Servings: 6 - 8

Ingredients:

4 large potatoes, chopped into 1" cubes

½ cup extra virgin olive oil

2 tsp powdered turmeric

½ cup lemon juice

1½ tsp sea salt

½ tsp cumin seeds (optional)

1 small red onion, finely diced

2 cloves of garlic, minced

2 tbsp fresh parsley (or preferred fresh herbs, chopped)

Directions:

1. Steam the potatoes for 10 to 15 minutes or until fork tender.

2. Mix the lemon juice, cumin seeds (if you like), turmeric and salt in small bowl.

3. Transfer the steamed potatoes to a large bowl then pour the lemon juice mixture over the potatoes.

4. Add the garlic and onions, then gently stir to coat the potatoes. Cover the bowl then refrigerate to cool.

5. Once the potatoes are cool, pour in the olive oil, add fresh herbs then stir properly.

6. Serve chilled or at room temperature.

Liver Friendly Greek Salad

Prep time: 40 minutes

Cooking time: 0 minute

Servings: 6

Ingredients:

For the salad:

1 unpeeled English cucumber (remove the seeds then slice into ¼" thickness)

1 seeded yellow bell pepper, big-chopped

1 seeded orange bell pepper, big-chopped

2 cups grape tomatoes, halved

½ red onion, sliced into half-circles

4 oz. feta cheese (optional)

½ cup black olives, pitted

For the vinaigrette:

½ cup original olive oil

¼ cup good red wine vinegar

2 cloves of garlic, minced

½ tsp Dijon mustard

1 tsp dried oregano

1 tsp kosher salt

½ tsp freshly ground black pepper

Directions:

1. In a large bowl, combine the cucumber, tomatoes, peppers and red onion.

2. In another bowl, whisk the garlic, mustard, oregano, vinegar, pepper and salt together. Emulsify the vinaigrette by slowly adding the olive oil while you whisk.

3. Pour the vinaigrette all over the veggies then add the feta (if using), olives and then lightly toss.

4. Let it sit for 30 minutes to allow the flavors to infuse into each other. Serve at room temperature.

Spinach-Tuna Salad

Preparation time: 10 minutes

Cooking time: 0 minute

Servings: 1

Ingredients:

2 cups baby spinach

1 (5 oz.) can chunk light tuna in water, drained

1½ tbsp water

1½ tbsp lemon juice

1 medium-sized peeled orange, sliced

4 pitted olives, diced

2 tbsp feta cheese

2 tbsp parsley

Directions:

1. In a bowl, mix the water and lemon juice together. Add the tuna, feta, olives and parsley; then stir to combine.

2. Serve tuna salad over 2 cups of spinach, with orange on the side. Enjoy!

Mediterranean Bean Salad

This quickie bean salad is easy to make and you can choose to add or omit any veggie.

Preparation time: 10 minutes

Cooking time: 0 minute

Servings: 1

Ingredients:

1 can garbanzo beans (drained and rinsed)

1 can red beans (drained and rinsed)

1 tomato, chopped

½ red onion, chopped

½ lemon juice

1 tbsp extra virgin olive oil

Salt to taste

Directions:

1. In a bowl, mix the garbanzo beans, red beans, tomato, red onion, lemon juice, olive oil and salt to taste. Serve.

Mediterranean-Style Cucumber Salad

Preparation time: 10 minute

Cooking time: 0 minute

Servings: 1

Ingredients:

1 large tomato

1 small cucumber

½ onion

¼ cup feta

Salt

Extra virgin olive oil

Olives (optional)

Directions:

1. In a bowl, mix cucumber, tomato, red pepper, onion and feta cheese.

2. Sprinkle a little bit of salt and a bit of extra virgin olive oil. Add a couple of olives for extra taste.

Poached Egg 'N' Lentil Salad

Preparation time: 10 minutes

Cooking time: 0 minute

Servings: 1

Ingredients:

1 cup cooked lentils

1 cup fresh baby spinach

1 poached egg

¼ avocado

½ tomato, chopped

Directions:

1. In a bowl, mix all the ingredients together. Serve with a slice of whole wheat toast. Enjoy!

Kelp Noodles Salad With Lime And Ginger

Preparation time: 15 minutes

Cooking time: 5 minutes

Servings: 2

Ingredients:

For the salad:

1 (16 oz.) pack of kelp noodles

¼ cup diced purple cabbage

1 avocado, chopped

¼ cup shredded carrots

1 large scallion, diced

For the Lime and Ginger Dressing:

1" piece ginger, minced

2 limes, juice

¼ cup extra virgin olive oil

2 tsp honey

1/8 tsp black pepper

1/8 tsp sea salt

Directions:

1. Soak the kelp noodles in warm water for about 5 minutes to make them soft then drain. 2. Make the noodles shorter by using a knife or kitchen shears.

3. Let the noodles cool then transfer to a salad bowl. Garnish with carrots, scallions, purple cabbage and avocado.

4. To prepare the dressing; combine all the ingredients in a jar with lid. Cover then shake properly until well mixed. Pour the dressing over the salad, mix until well coated.

Ginger Flavored Bean 'N' Carrot Salad
Preparation time: 10 minutes

Cooking time: 0 minute

Servings: 4

Ingredients:

For the salad:

1 cup of fresh bean sprouts

3 medium carrots, roughly grated

2 tbsp sesame seeds (slightly dry roasted)

For the dressing:

1 dessert spoon peanut oil

¼ cup fresh lemon juice

1 dessert spoon sesame oil

4 tsp palm/brown sugar

3 tsp finely grated fresh ginger

Freshly ground black pepper

Directions:

1. In a bowl, mix all the dressing ingredients then pour over the salad ingredients

2. Combine by tossing. Serve with cold or grilled meat.

DRINKS, SMOOTHIES AND SHAKES RECIPES

Nature Detox Licorice Tea

Preparation time: 10 minutes

Cooking time: 15 minutes

Servings: 4 to 6

Ingredients:

2½ tsp dried licorice root

½ cup dried peppermint leaves, crushed

1 cinnamon stick

4 sprigs of fresh mint for taste

½ cup raw honey

6 cups of water

Directions:

1. In a large pot, boil 6 cups of water then in the licorice and cinnamon.

2. Simmer for about 15 minutes, covering the pot partially. Remove the pot from heat then blend the peppermint leaves with other ingredients.

3. Steep for 10 minutes then strain the tea by pressing on the herbs in order to extract enough nutrients.

4. Add honey then stir until it dissolves.

5. Let it sit for about 1 hour before drinking. Serve hot or chilled.

Olive And Clover Leaf Detox Tea

Preparation time: 10 minutes

Cooking time: 15 minutes

Servings: 3

Ingredients:

1 tsp nettles

1 tsp red clover blossoms

1 tsp olive leaf

½ tsp licorice root

½ tsp chickweed

½ tsp fennel seeds

3 cups of boiling water

Directions:

1. Crush all the ingredients then boil for about 15 minutes.

2. Steep then strain. Serve.

Herby Lemon Cleansing Smoothie

This smoothie contains the natural nutrients of citrus fruit. It helps cleanse the liver and also boost the immune system.

Preparation time: 10 minutes

Cooking time: 0 minute

Servings: 2

Ingredients:

3 lemons

5 stalks of celery

1 cup of chopped parsley

2 cups of water

Directions:

1. Combine all ingredients in your blender then blend until it incorporates.

2. Drink 2 cups before each main meal.

Lemony Cleansing Papaya Smoothie

This smoothie contains papaya which aids digestion and improve the liver function.

Preparation time: 10 minutes

Cooking time: 0 minute

Servings: 1

Ingredients:

½ of papaya

½ lemon, juice

1 cup of water

Directions:

1. Combine all the ingredients in a blender then process until smooth.

2. Drink smoothie on an empty stomach for seven days in a row.

Cabbage - Carrot Liver Detox Smoothie

This smoothie is combination of two power-pack fruits 'carrots and red cabbage' which is great for cleansing the liver of any toxin and improves the liver performance.

Preparation time: 10 minutes

Cooking time: 0 minute

Servings: 1

Ingredients:

1 cup of carrot juice

3 leaves of red cabbage

Directions:

1. Combine the ingredients in a blender then process until smooth.

2. Serve chilled and preferable on an empty stomach.

3. Drink smoothie for at least 7 days in a row, 2 times a month.

Cranberry-Beet Liver Cleansing Smoothie

This smoothie fill packed with vitamins and antioxidants which stimulates and cleanses the liver.

Preparation time: 10 minutes

Cooking time: 0 minute

Servings: 1

Ingredients:

½ cup of cranberries

3 beets

1 lemon, juice

Ice or cold water

Directions:

1. Place the beets including the skin and all in a juicer then extract the resulting liquid.

2. Pour the cranberries and lemon juice into a blender then process well mixed.

3. Add the beet juice then process for a couple of seconds.

4. Drink smoothie on an empty stomach.

Carrot-Beetroot Detox Juice

Preparation time: 10 minutes

Cooking time: 0 minute

Servings: 1

Ingredients:

1 carrot

1 beet

1/3 - ½ cup parsley

1 lemon, peeled

Directions:

1. Combine all ingredients in a juicer the process. Enjoy.

Liver Cleansing Green Drink

Preparation time: 10 minutes

Cooking time: 0 minute

Servings: 1

Ingredients:

2 cups kale

½ of cucumber

½ lemon, peeled

1 lime, peeled

1 cup Swiss chard

Directions:

1. Process all the ingredients through a juicer. Enjoy.

Green Liver Detox Smoothie

Preparation time: 10 minutes

Cooking time: 0 minutes

Servings: 1

Ingredients:

½ cup dandelion greens (or preferred bitter green)

1 peeled lemon

2 peeled oranges

½ rib celery

½ cup parsley

Directions:

1. Combine all the ingredients in a blender then process until smooth. Enjoy!

Liver Cleansing Veggie Smoothie

Preparation time: 10 minutes

Cooking time: 0 minute

Servings: 2

Ingredients:

¼ of avocado (chopped and frozen)

1 small green apple (chopped and frozen)

1 zucchini (chopped and frozen)

1 cup mixed greens (like watercress, broccoli florets, silver beet, beetroot greens, spinach or kale)

1 tsp chia seeds

¼ cup parsley and/or coriander

2 cups coconut water

¼ tsp ground turmeric

½ lemon, juiced

Directions:

1. Combine all the ingredients in the blender then blitz on high setting for 30 seconds or until smooth.

2. Transfer into two glasses then serve.

Cooking tip: For a creamy smoothie, substitute half of the coconut water for your preferred choice of milk.

Fatty Liver Iced Tea

Preparation time: 10 minutes

Cooking time: 0 minute

Servings: 12

Ingredients:

3 lemons, juice

4 Detox tea bags

2 peppermint tea bags

2 hibiscus tea bags (optional)

2 ginger tea bags

1 milk thistle tea bag

For serving: honey, fresh mint (optional)

Directions:

1. Place all the tea bags in a large pitcher.

2. Boil 4 cups water then pour it into the pitcher containing the tea bags.

3. Steep for 10 to 15 minutes. Pour the tea into the pitcher then you're left with tea bags.

4. Pour more boiling water into the pitcher and repeat steeping process for a total of 3 times.

5. When you've made the tea 3 times, you'll have a large amount of about 12 cups of tea.

 6. Add the fresh lemon juice then allow cooling or refrigerating immediately to cool.

7. Pour tea over ice and serve with fresh mint, once a day.

Banana, Cherry And Berry Smoothie

Preparation time: 5 minutes

Cooking time: 0 minute

Servings: 1

Ingredients:

8 oz. filtered water

1 large peeled banana

1 cup fresh or frozen cherries

1 cup organic strawberries

Directions:

1. Pour the liquid into your blender then followed by soft fruits.

2. Process on high setting for 30 seconds or until creamy. Enjoy!

DESEERTS RECIPES

Almond Coated French Toast

Preparation time: 10 minutes

Cooking time: 15 to 17 minutes

Servings: 6

Ingredients:

1 tbsp butter

6 eggs

1½ cup low fat milk

4 tbsp honey

1½ tsp vanilla extract

1 loaf of day old bread, sliced

2 tsp salt

1 tsp orange zest

½ cup slivered almonds (placed on a flat plate)

Optional toppings: powdered sugar, squeeze of orange juice, fresh berries.

Directions:

1. Beat eggs, honey, milk, vanilla, orange zest and salt together.

2. Place the bread slices on a shallow baking pan then pour the mixture all over the top of the bread.

3. Let each side soak for 2 minutes, while you preheat a large skillet to medium.

4. Melt the butter in heated pan then dip one side of each slice of soaked bread in slivered almonds for a nice coating.

5. Place bread slices in the pan one after the other, working in batches.

6. Sauté each side of the bread for about 3 minutes, until golden brown, then transfer to a pan in oven until you're ready to serve.

7. Garnish with fresh berries, orange juice and powdered sugar, if desired.

Stone Baked Fruits

Preparation time: 10 minutes

Cooking time: 15 minutes

Servings: 4

Ingredients:

2 tbsp cold no-salt-added butter, small cubes

2 pitted apricots, sliced into thick slices

2 pitted peaches, sliced into thick slices

2 pitted plums, sliced into thick slices

2 pitted nectarines, sliced into thick slices

½ cup apple juice

2 tbsp honey

1 tbsp lemon zest (optional)

1 tbsp grated ginger (optional)

Directions:

1. Preheat the oven to 400°F.

2. In a small 4 by 6" casserole dish, alternate the layers of fruit slices, slightly overlapping until the dish is full and covered.

3. Add butter on top then drizzle equally with honey.

4. Pour the apple juice all over the whole dish then allow it to soak as the oven preheats. Sprinkle with grated ginger and lemon zest if you like.

5. Bake for about 15 minutes or until it forms a slight char on the outer rims of each fruit slice.

6. Turn off the heat then let it rest in oven for 5 minutes.

7. Take out the baked fruits from the oven then let it cool for about 10 minutes.

Cooking tip: You can add maple syrup and lemon zest over the apples and pears or lime zest and agave nectar over pineapple, papaya and mango.

Savory Spinach - Mushroom Muffins

Preparation time: 20 minutes

Cooking time: 35 minutes

Servings: 24 muffins

Ingredients:

1½ cups self-rising whole-meal flour

1 ½ -2 oz. cooked spinach, chopped

1 egg

5 button mushrooms, finely diced

1 cup +2 tsp soy milk

2.5 oz. firm tofu, diced

3 tbsp shallots, diced

3.4 oz. olive oil

2 tbsp sunflower seeds

1 tsp salt

Directions:

1. Preheat the oven to374°F.

2. Whisk the egg. Pour into the flour, then stir in other ingredients

3. Scoop batter into oiled muffin tins

4. Bake for 35 minutes, until golden brown

5. Serve hot with homemade carrot, pumpkin and potato soup.

Note: Muffins can be stored in an air-tight container

Chocolate Cranberry Bark
This dessert is rich in antioxidant and helps to fuel your metabolism.

Preparation time: 10 minutes

Cooking time: 30 minutes

Servings: 12 pieces

Ingredients:

½ cup coconut oil, melted

½ cup cocoa powder or cacao

¼ cup melted honey

¼ cup roasted pecan pieces

¼ cup dried cranberries

Pinch of sea salt

Directions:

1. In a bowl, mix the cacao or cocoa powder, coconut oil and honey together.

2. Pour the mixture into a baking paper or foil lined baking tray. Smooth it out evenly.

3. Sprinkle the remaining ingredients equally over the chocolate mixture.

4. Place the tray into the freezer for 30 minutes to set.

5. Break up the bark then store in an airtight container in the fridge.

Sweet Cinnamon Applesauce

This is an amazing dessert and also liver friendly.

Preparation time: 10 minutes

Cooking time: 40 minutes

Servings: 4

Ingredients:

3 lbs peeled apples, sliced

2 tbsp coconut oil or ghee, melted

¼ cup water

½ tsp ground cloves

1 tsp fresh lemon juice

Honey or stevia, to taste (optional)

2 tsp cinnamon

Directions:

1. Preheat the oven to 425°F.

2. Assemble all the ingredients in a large baking dish.

3. Bake for about 40 minutes, or until the apples become very soft. The baking time depends on how thin the apples slices are.

4. Once done, pour the mixture into a food processor or blender then process until smooth.

5. Store in a glass jar in the fridge.

Banana Peanut Butter Cake

Preparation time: 20 minutes

Cooking time: 1 hour

Servings: 2 to 4

Ingredients:

1 tsp baking powder

4 eggs, beaten

4 mashed over-ripe bananas

½ cup peanut butter

4 tbsp coconut oil, softened

1 tsp cinnamon

½ cup almond meal

¼ cup diced pecans

1 tsp ground cloves

1 tsp baking soda

Directions:

1. Preheat the oven to 350°F. Pour the mashed bananas, peanut butter and eggs into a blender then process until smooth.

2. In a bowl, combine all the ingredients then mix properly with your hand until combined.

3. Pour the mixture into an oiled cake tin then bake for about 1 hour, or until a toothpick inserted comes out clean.

4. Store cake in an airtight container in the fridge.

Creamy Maple Bran Oats

Preparation time: 20 minutes

Cooking time: 7 minutes

Servings: 4

Ingredients:

½ cup rolled oats

½ cup oat bran

1¼ cups almond milk

¼ cup Greek yogurt (or 1-2 tbsp chia seeds)

¼ tsp salt

½ tsp vanilla

½ - 1 tsp cinnamon

1 tbsp honey or maple syrup

8 drops liquid stevia

Fresh or spiced peaches

1 peach, thinly sliced

1 - 2 tbsp coconut oil

½ tsp cinnamon

1 tsp maple syrup

1/16 tsp salt

Directions:

1. Mix the rolled oats, oat bran, almond milk, Greek yogurt or chia seeds, salt, vanilla, cinnamon, honey or maple syrup and liquid stevia together then let it sit in the fridge, covered, overnight.

2. In a small pan, heat oil, add cinnamon, maple syrup, peaches and salt. Stir then sauté for about 5 to 7 minutes.

3. Remove from heat then freeze for some minutes to speed up cooling.

4. For two servings, scoop about half of the overnight oats (¼ cup for each glass) into two glasses.

5. Top with a spoonful of the peach mixture then top with preferred granola. Repeat this process for additional serving.

Note: You can make two small parfaits from this recipe or a large single one.

Mini Banana Pudding

Preparation time: 20 minutes

Cooking time: 25 minutes

Servings: 3

Ingredients:

2 bananas, sliced thinly

¾ cup low fat milk

10 whole almonds

1 tbsp honey

2 tbsp cornstarch

1/16 tsp sea or kosher salt

1 egg yolk, slightly whisked

½ tsp vanilla

6 (4 oz.) dessert dishes

Directions:

1. Preheat the oven to 325°F. Roast the almonds for 12 minutes then let it cool, while you prepare the pudding.

2. Once cooled, mince the almonds with a knife or in a blender.

3. Combine cornstarch, salt and honey in a saucepan. Add the egg yolk then stir in milk gradually.

4. Continue stirring until well mixed. Turn the heat to medium heat and stir constantly while cooking.

5. Continue cooking until you get a pudding like texture.

6. Remove from heat then stir in vanilla.

7. While the pudding is still warm, alternate it with bananas in the dessert dishes. Sprinkle the minced almonds on top then top with whipped topping if you like.

The End

Made in United States
Orlando, FL
16 August 2022

21107551R00055